Guide to WordPress

Simple guide to get to know WordPress

V. Telman

Copyright © 2024

Guide to WordPress

1.Introduction

WordPress is an open-source content management platform (CMS) used by millions of people worldwide to create and manage websites of all kinds. It was launched in 2003 as a platform for blog creation, but over the years it has evolved into a complete solution for creating websites of any size and complexity.

WordPress is extremely flexible and allows users to customize their website according to their needs, thanks to a wide range of themes and plugins available. Its intuitive and easy-to-use interface makes it suitable for both beginners and experts, allowing anyone to create a professional website without the need for advanced technical knowledge.

In this introduction to WordPress, we will explore its key features, the advantages it offers compared to other platforms, and how to get started using it to create your website.

You will discover that WordPress is the ideal choice for anyone looking to create a visually appealing, functional, and search engine optimized website.

Key Features of WordPress

WordPress offers a variety of features that set it apart from other content management platforms on the market. Here are some of its key features:

1. Ease of use: one of the main reasons WordPress is so popular is its intuitive and easy-to-use interface. Even beginners can learn how to use it quickly, thanks to a clear and well-organized control panel.

2. Customization: WordPress allows users to customize their website using themes and plugins. Themes allow you to modify the aesthetic appearance of the site, while plugins add extra functionality, such as contact forms,

photo galleries, e-commerce, and more.

3. SEO-friendly: WordPress is optimized for search engines, which means that websites created with this platform are more likely to be well-positioned in search results. Additionally, there are numerous plugins available to further improve the SEO optimization of your site.

4. Scalability: WordPress can handle websites of any size, from small blogs to large corporate portals. Thanks to its modular architecture, you can add new features at any time without compromising the site's performance.

5. Active Community: WordPress has a large and vibrant community of developers, designers, and users who contribute to its constant evolution. This means you can easily find answers to your questions and technical support, as well as stay up to date on the latest news and trends in web design.

Advantages of WordPress Compared to Other Platforms

WordPress offers numerous advantages over other content management platforms available on the market. Here are some of the main advantages of WordPress:

1. Open source: WordPress is open-source software, which means it is free to download, use, and modify. This allows you to save on website development and customization costs compared to proprietary solutions.

2. Wide choice of themes and plugins: WordPress offers a wide range of free and paid themes and plugins, allowing you to customize your website according to your needs and preferences. No matter what type of site you want to create, you will surely find a theme and plugin that suits you.

3. Security: WordPress is constantly updated to ensure the maximum security of websites created with this platform. Additionally, there are numerous plugins available to enhance your site's security, such as automatic backups, antivirus, and firewalls.

4. Multilingual support: WordPress natively supports internationalization, allowing you to easily create multilingual websites. This is particularly useful for businesses operating globally or wishing to reach a wide international audience.

5. Centralized content management: WordPress allows you to manage all your website content from a single platform, without the need for third-party tools. You can easily add, edit, or delete pages, articles, images, and more, all from the WordPress control panel.

Getting Started with WordPress

Now that you have seen the features and advantages of WordPress, it's time to start using it to create your website. Here is a step-by-step guide on how to get started with WordPress:

1. Purchase a domain and hosting: Before you can install WordPress, you need to purchase a domain name and hosting service for your website. The domain name is your website's web address (e.g., www.mygreatwebsite.com), while hosting service is the space on a server hosting your site's files. There are numerous domain and hosting providers available on the market, so do some research to find the best solution for you.

2. Install WordPress: Many hosting providers offer one-click WordPress installations, making the process extremely simple and fast. Alternatively, you can download the WordPress software from the official site and install it manually on your server. Follow the hosting provider's instructions or online

guides to successfully complete the installation.

3. Choose a theme: Once WordPress is installed, you can start customizing your website by choosing a theme. WordPress offers a wide selection of free and paid themes that you can customize to your taste and brand style. Explore the available options and choose the theme that best suits your needs.

4. Add content: Now that you have selected your site's theme, it's time to add content. Create pages for the main sections of the site, such as the homepage, about us, services, contacts, and so on. Complete the site with articles, images, videos, and other elements you want to share with your visitors.

5. Install plugins: To enhance your site's functionality, you can install additional plugins available on WordPress. Check out the official plugin repository to find those that best suit your needs, such as SEO plugins,

security plugins, photo galleries, contact forms, and more.

6. Optimize for search engines: To ensure your site is well-positioned in search results, make sure to optimize it for search engines. Use SEO plugins like Yoast SEO to optimize your site's content, meta tags, permalinks, and more, to maximize your site's online visibility.

7. Keep the site updated: Finally, make sure to regularly update WordPress, themes, and plugins on your website to ensure maximum security and performance. Monitor the site to ensure everything is working correctly and address any issues or errors as soon as possible.

WordPress is a flexible, powerful, and easy-to-use content management platform that allows you to create professional and attractive websites quickly and efficiently. With a wide selection of themes and plugins available, WordPress allows you to customize your website according to your needs, regardless of the industry you operate in.

2. Installing Wordpress on your own server

WordPress is a blogging and content management platform that allows users to create and maintain a website easily and effectively. Installing WordPress on your own server is a relatively simple process, but it does require some technical knowledge. In this detailed guide, I will explain step by step how to install WordPress on your server.

Before starting, it is important to make sure you have everything you need for the WordPress installation. You will need a web server such as Apache, Nginx, or Microsoft IIS, a MySQL, MariaDB, or SQLite database, and a PHP server. Make sure you also have access to the administration panel of your server to properly configure WordPress.

Step 1: Download WordPress

The first step to installing WordPress on your server is to download the latest version of the software from the official website wordpress.org. Once you have downloaded the zip file, extract it into the public folder of your web server. You can do this via FTP or through your server's control panel, depending on your preferences and technical knowledge.

Step 2: Configure the database

After extracting the WordPress files into your server's folder, you will need to create a database for your site. Access your server's administration panel and create a new database, making sure to store the access details (database name, username, and password) in a secure location. These details will be needed during the WordPress installation.

Step 3: Configure the wp-config.php file

Once the database is created, you will need to configure the wp-config.php file of WordPress with the database access details. To do this, copy the wp-config-sample.php file from the WordPress folder and rename it to wp-config.php. Open the file with a text editor and enter the database details you created earlier.

Save the wp-config.php file and close it. This file contains the database access settings for WordPress and allows the software to connect correctly to the database during installation and use.

Step 4: Run the WordPress installation

Now you are ready to run the WordPress installation on your server. Open your preferred web browser and visit your website's URL. You will be guided through the WordPress installation process, which involves configuring basic site information such as the title, description, administrator email address, and password to access the admin area.

During the installation, you will be asked to enter the database details you configured in the wp-config.php file. Make sure to correctly enter the database name, username, and password to connect to the database.

Once the installation is complete, you can access the WordPress administration area and start customizing your website. You can change the theme, add new content, install plugins, and much more to create a unique and personalized website.

Step 5: Add an SSL certificate (optional)

To ensure the security of your website and your visitors, I recommend adding an SSL certificate to your server. This encrypts communications between the visitor's browser and your website, ensuring the confidentiality and integrity of transmitted data.

You can get a free SSL certificate from Let's Encrypt or purchase one from an SSL certificate provider. After installing and configuring the SSL certificate on your server, make sure to set up WordPress to use HTTPS instead of HTTP for secure connections.

Conclusion

Installing WordPress on your own server may seem complicated, but with this detailed guide, I hope I have helped you understand the necessary steps to successfully complete the installation. Remember that it is important to carefully follow each step and make sure you have all the necessary requirements before starting.

Once WordPress is installed, you will have a powerful tool to create and manage your website easily and effectively. Take advantage of exploring the various features offered by WordPress and customize your website according to your needs and preferences.

3. Initial Configuration of WordPress

WordPress is one of the most popular blogging platforms in the world, used by millions of people to create successful websites and blogs. When starting to use WordPress for the first time, it is important to perform the initial configuration to ensure that the site functions properly and is optimized for long-term success. In this article, we will explore step by step how to configure WordPress to achieve the best possible results.

Step 1: Install WordPress

The first step in configuring WordPress is to install the platform on the web server. There are several ways to install WordPress, but one of the most common is using a web hosting service that offers one-click installation. Many hosting companies such as Bluehost, SiteGround, and HostGator offer this service, making the installation of WordPress a simple and quick task.

Once WordPress is installed on the web

server, you can access the administration panel using the credentials provided during the installation. The administration panel is the central hub of the website and allows you to manage all aspects of the site, including content, themes, plugins, and settings.

Step 2: Configure General Settings

After logging into the WordPress administration panel, it is important to configure the general settings of the site. To do this, click on "Settings" in the left sidebar and select "General." In this section, you can set the site title, description, site URL, and other basic information.

It is important to pay special attention to the site URL and make sure it is correct. If you want to use www in your URL, make sure to add www. to the main domain. You can also set the time zone and date and time format in this section.

Step 3: Configure Writing and Reading Settings

After configuring the general settings, it is also important to configure the writing and reading settings. To do this, click on "Settings" in the left sidebar and select "Writing." In this section, you can set the default format for new content and the remote publishing service, if desired.

Next, click on "Settings" and select "Reading." In this section, you can set the default page of the website, the display of RSS feeds, and other reading options. For example, you can set a static page as the homepage instead of the list of the most recent posts.

Step 4: Configure Discussion and Media Settings

After configuring the writing and reading settings, it's time to configure the discussion and media settings. To do this, click on "Settings" in the left sidebar and select "Discussion." In this section, you can set the comment moderation settings, the word limit in discussions, and other discussion options.

Next, click on "Settings" and select "Media." In this section, you can set the default sizes for images uploaded to the website, the path for attachments, and other media options.

Step 5: Install a Theme

One of the most important aspects of the initial configuration of WordPress is installing a theme. Themes are the design of the website and determine the look and functionality of the site. WordPress offers a wide range of free and premium themes to choose from, which you can install directly from the administration panel.

To install a theme, click on "Appearance" in the left sidebar and select "Themes." In this section, you can search for free themes available on WordPress.org or upload a premium theme purchased from another source. Once the theme is installed, you can activate it and customize it to fit your needs.

Step 6: Install Plugins

In addition to installing a theme, it is

important to also install plugins to expand the functionality of the website. Plugins are small programs that add new features to the site and help optimize performance. WordPress offers a wide range of free and premium plugins to choose from, which you can install directly from the administration panel.

To install a plugin, click on "Plugins" in the left sidebar and select "Add new." In this section, you can search for free plugins available on WordPress.org or upload a premium plugin purchased from another source. Once the plugin is installed, you can activate it and configure it as desired.

Step 7: Optimize the Site for Search Engines

Finally, it is important to optimize the site for search engines to ensure that it is ranked on search engines like Google and Bing. There are several actions you can take to optimize the site for search engines, such as creating XML sitemaps, optimizing meta tags, and using relevant keywords in the content.

To create an XML sitemap, you can use a

plugin like Yoast SEO or All in One SEO Pack. These plugins allow you to automatically generate an XML sitemap of the website that can be submitted to search engines to index the site's pages. It is also important to use relevant meta tags such as title, description, and keywords in the content to help search engines understand what the website is about.

Conclusion

Properly configuring WordPress is essential to ensure the long-term success of the website. By following the steps described above, you can configure WordPress optimally and achieve the best possible results. Once the site is configured, it is important to regularly update the site and monitor performance to ensure that you provide visitors with a high-quality experience.

4. How to use Gutenberg

Gutenberg is the WordPress editor that allows you to create visually appealing content in a simple and intuitive way. In this article, I will show you how to use all of its features to create high-quality pages and articles for your website.

First of all, it is important to make sure you have installed and activated the Gutenberg plugin on your WordPress site. Once you have done this, you can start creating your content using the Gutenberg editor.

When you create a new page or article, you will see a clean and minimalist interface that allows you to focus on creating your content. In the center of the editor, you will find a writing area where you can start typing your text. You can also add new blocks by clicking on the "+" button located at the top left of the editor.

Blocks are the main feature of Gutenberg and allow you to insert different types of content into your page or article. For example, you can add text blocks, images, videos, galleries, buttons, quotes, tables, and much more. Each block can be customized to suit your needs, allowing you to edit the text, size, color, and style of the content.

To add a block, click on the "+" button and select the type of block you want to add. Once you have added the block, you can start entering your content inside it. You can also move blocks by dragging them with the mouse or delete a block by clicking on the trash icon that appears when you hover over the block.

In addition to basic blocks, Gutenberg also offers the option to use reusable blocks and custom blocks. Reusable blocks allow you to save a custom block and reuse it on other pages or articles. To create a reusable block, select an existing block and click on the ellipsis icon that appears at the top right of the block. Select "Add to reusable blocks" and assign a name to your reusable block. Once saved, you can find the reusable block in the "Reusable blocks" section of the block menu

5.The Media Library

A media library in WordPress is an essential tool for users who want to easily manage and organize multimedia files within their website. This feature allows users to easily upload, view, edit, and delete images, videos, audio, and other types of multimedia files directly from the WordPress control panel.

Once logged into the WordPress admin panel, users can access the media library by clicking on the "Library" icon in the left sidebar. Inside the media library, users can view all the multimedia files uploaded to the website, including images, videos, audio, and other file types.

The WordPress media library offers several features that greatly simplify the management of multimedia files on the website. Key features include the ability to upload new multimedia files, organize files into folders, and insert multimedia files directly into website pages and posts.

To upload a new multimedia file, simply click on the "Add new" button above the media library. From here, users can select the desired multimedia file from their computer and upload it to the website. Once the file is uploaded, users can edit the title, description, and copyright information directly from the media library.

To organize multimedia files within the media library, users can create custom folders and assign files to the desired folders. This allows users to keep multimedia files organized and easily accessible for future use.

In addition to managing multimedia files, the WordPress media library also allows users to insert multimedia files directly into website pages and posts. To do this, simply open the desired page or post and click on the "Add media" button. From here, users can select the multimedia file to insert and customize the display settings.

Furthermore, the WordPress media library also offers advanced features for editing and optimizing multimedia files. Users can edit images to resize them, crop them, or adjust brightness and contrast. Additionally, users can optimize multimedia files to reduce size and improve website loading speeds.

In conclusion, the WordPress media library is an essential tool for users who want to easily manage and organize multimedia files on their website. With advanced features for uploading, organizing, inserting, and editing multimedia files, the WordPress media library is a valuable ally in ensuring efficient and professional management of multimedia content on the website.

6.Creating a website with Wordpress

Wordpress is one of the most popular platforms for creating websites, thanks to its ease of use and numerous features. In this article, I will guide you step by step in creating your first website with Wordpress.

Step 1: Purchase a domain and hosting

The first step in creating your website with Wordpress is to purchase a domain and hosting service. The domain is the address of your website (e.g. www.mywebsite.com), while hosting is the space where your website will be stored.

There are many companies that offer hosting and domain services, so you can choose the one that best fits your needs and budget. After purchasing the domain and hosting, you will have access to your account control panel, where you can install Wordpress.

Step 2 if not yet done: Install Wordpress

Once you have purchased the domain and hosting, it's time to install Wordpress on your server. Most hosting providers offer a one-click installation of Wordpress, which allows you to install the platform in just a few minutes.

After installing Wordpress, you can access the administration panel of your website, called Dashboard. Here you can manage all aspects of your website, such as creating pages, editing content, and installing themes and plugins.

Step 3: Choose a theme

The theme is the design of your website. Wordpress offers a wide range of free and paid themes that you can use to customize the look of your website.

You can choose a theme that fits your industry and style, and is easy to customize. Once you have selected the theme, you can further customize it by changing colors, font sizes, and adding your logo.

Step 4: Create website pages

Your website will need several pages to present your content in an organized way. The most common pages are the homepage, contact page, About Us page, and product or service pages.

To create a new page in Wordpress, go to the Pages menu in your Dashboard and click on Add New. Here you can enter the title and content of the page, which can be enriched with text, images, and videos.

Step 5: Add content

Now that you have created the pages of your website, it's time to add your content. Write original and quality text that describes your business, products, or services, and use high-quality images to enhance your content.

You can also create a blog on your website to share news, articles, and useful resources with your visitors. The blog is a great tool to improve the ranking of your website on search engines and to offer your visitors fresh and interesting content.

Step 6: Install plugins

Plugins are extensions that add extra functionality to your website. Wordpress offers a wide range of free and paid plugins that you can install to improve the performance of your website and add new features.

Some essential plugins for your website are SEO (search engine optimization), security, backup, and social media sharing plugins. You can install plugins directly from the Plugin menu in your Dashboard.

Step 7: Optimize your website for search engines

To improve the ranking of your website on search engines, it is important to optimize the content and structure of the site for search engines. Use the most important keywords for your industry in the titles, subtitles, and text of your website, and create a clear and well-organized site structure.

You can use an SEO plugin like Yoast SEO to optimize your content and improve the visibility of your website on search engines.

Step 8: Test and optimize your website

Once you have completed creating your website with Wordpress, it is important to test the site and optimize it to improve its performance. Check that all pages are correctly displayed and that links are working, and ensure that the site loads quickly on all devices.

You can use tools like Google PageSpeed Insights and GTmetrix to check the performance of your website and identify areas for improvement.

Conclusion

Creating the first website with Wordpress may seem complex, but by following this step-by-step guide, you can create a professional and functional website in no time. Wordpress offers a wide range of features and customizations that will allow you to create a unique and successful website.

Remember to regularly update your website with fresh and quality content, and monitor the site's performance to ensure it is always at its best.

7.Content Management: Creating Pages and Articles

Content management is a fundamental aspect of any website or blomg, as it determines the quality and relevance of the messages conveyed to visitors. Thanks to the Wordpress platform, it is possible to effectively manage the creation of pages, articles, and other types of content in an intuitive and fast way.

Wordpress is one of the most widely used Content Management Systems (CMS) in the world, used by millions of websites of various sizes and sectors. One of the main features of Wordpress is its flexibility and customizability, allowing users to create and manage content in a simple and immediate way, without the need to know specific programming languages.

Creating pages and articles with Wordpress is a very easy and intuitive process. To get started, simply access the website's control panel and select the content section. Here you will find all the options to create new articles, pages, categories, and tags, as well as organize the site's menu.

The creation of pages and articles is done through a text editor similar to a word processor, which allows you to format content, insert images, links, and other multimedia elements. Thanks to the wide range of plugins available for Wordpress, it is possible to add extra functionality to the editor to make content creation easier and faster.

One of the most useful features of Wordpress is the ability to schedule the publication of articles and pages in advance. This way, you can prepare content in advance and schedule publication based on specific dates and times.

Wordpress also offers the ability to manage comments on content, allowing users to interact and leave feedback on website pages and articles. It is possible to moderate comments, approve or reject them, and manage privacy and security settings to protect the site from spam and cyber attacks.

To optimize content for search engines,

Wordpress offers a series of tools for Search Engine Optimization (SEO). You can insert keywords, meta descriptions, tags, and other useful information to improve the website's positioning on search engines and increase online visibility.

Furthermore, Wordpress allows you to create responsive pages and articles, optimized to be viewed on mobile devices such as smartphones and tablets. Thanks to the responsive themes available for Wordpress, you can ensure an optimal browsing experience for users visiting the site from different devices.

Content management with Wordpress is a continuous and dynamic process that requires consistency and attention to keep the website updated and interesting for visitors. Thanks to the advanced features and ease of use of the platform, it is possible to create and manage high-quality pages and articles effectively, allowing effective communication with the target audience and achieving the set goals for the website.

In conclusion, content management with Wordpress is an essential tool for anyone who needs to create and manage online content quickly and effectively. Wordpress offers a wide range of features and tools to facilitate the creation and management of pages, articles, and other types of content, allowing effective communication with the target audience and achieving tangible results on the web.

8. Customizing the site appearance with themes and layouts

With Wordpress, there is the possibility to easily customize the appearance of the site using predefined or custom themes and layouts. In this article, we will explore how to customize the appearance of your Wordpress site using the available themes and layouts.

Wordpress themes

A Wordpress theme is a set of files that determines the visual appearance of your site. Themes can be downloaded for free or purchased from various online sources. Wordpress offers a wide range of free themes in its official repository, but if you desire a more personalized design, you may opt for a premium theme.

To install a new Wordpress theme on your site, log in to the Wordpress dashboard and go to "Appearance" -> "Themes". From here, you can choose to install a theme from those available in the official repository, or you can upload a custom theme in ZIP format. Once you have installed the theme, you can activate it by clicking "Activate", and your site will immediately take on the new appearance of the selected theme.

Each Wordpress theme has a set of customization options that allow you to modify the appearance of the site without having to write any code. You can adjust colors, typography, layout, and other design details directly from the theme interface. Furthermore, many premium themes offer advanced features such as integration of plugins for creating photo galleries, image sliders, or contact forms.

Custom layout

In addition to choosing a theme, you can further customize the appearance of your Wordpress site by modifying the page layout. Wordpress provides the option to create pages and publish content flexibly through a visual text editor. However, if you desire more control over the look of your page, you may want to use a custom layout creation tool like

Elementor or Visual Composer.

Elementor is a popular Wordpress plugin that allows you to create complex page layouts visually by dragging and dropping elements onto your page. You can add columns, rows, text, images, videos, and much more without needing to write any code. Elementor offers a wide range of pre-designed templates that you can use as a starting point for your design, or you can start from scratch and create a completely custom layout.

Visual Composer is another very popular layout creation tool for Wordpress, with similar features to Elementor. Visual Composer also allows you to create complex page layouts visually, with the ability to customize every detail of the design. Visual Composer also offers a vast catalog of pre-designed elements that you can use to enhance your design, such as buttons, icons, sliders, and much more.

Both custom layout creation tools are very intuitive and easy to use, even for those with no programming knowledge. With Elementor or Visual Composer, you can create unique and original page layouts for your Wordpress site that perfectly fit your brand and style.

Conclusion

Customizing the appearance of your Wordpress site is a crucial step in creating a unique and professional website. With custom themes and layouts, you can quickly transform the look of your site without having to deal with complicated web development processes. Choose a theme that suits your style and needs, and use a custom layout creation tool to bring your creative vision to life.

Remember that customizing the site appearance is only part of the equation: always make sure to also focus on the content of your site, providing relevant and quality information to your visitors. With a well-designed and curated website, you will be able to effectively promote your brand online and successfully reach your target audience.

9. Using plugins to add functionality to the website

WordPress is one of the most popular platforms for creating websites. Its flexibility and ease of use make it ideal for people of all skill levels, from beginners to experts. One of the features that make WordPress so popular is the ability to add extra functionality to the website through the use of plugins. Plugins are small programs that extend the capabilities of the basic WordPress software, allowing you to customize and optimize the site according to your needs.

Plugins can be used for a wide range of purposes, such as optimizing the site for search engines, adding e-commerce functionality, creating image galleries, integrating with social media, and much more. In this article, we will explore how to use plugins to add functionality to the site with WordPress.

First of all, it is important to understand that plugins are essential for enhancing the user experience on the site and making it more effective. With over 55,000 plugins available on the official WordPress repository, there is a wide range of options to choose from to meet the specific needs of the site.

To install a new plugin on WordPress, simply access the site's administration panel and click on "Plugin" in the left-hand list. From here, you can search for a specific plugin or browse categories to discover new ones. Once you have found the desired plugin, simply click on "Install" and then on "Activate" to enable it on the site.

Now that the plugin is active, you can configure it according to your preferences. Some plugins have an intuitive user interface that allows you to easily customize settings, while others may require a bit more technical knowledge. It is important to carefully read the plugin documentation to understand how to use it effectively.

WordPress plugins can be divided into different categories based on the functionalities they offer. Some of the most popular ones include SEO plugins, which help optimize the site for search engines and improve its ranking in search results. Examples of SEO plugins are Yoast SEO and Rank Math.

Social media plugins are another popular category, which allows you to integrate social media profiles into the website and facilitate content sharing. Some examples of social media plugins are Social Media Share Buttons & Social Sharing Icons and AddToAny Share Buttons.

Caching plugins are useful for improving site performance by reducing page loading times. Examples of caching plugins are WP Super Cache and W3 Total Cache.

E-commerce plugins are essential for those

who want to sell products or services online. WooCommerce is one of the most popular e-commerce plugins for WordPress, allowing you to easily create a complete online store with all the necessary features.

Security plugins are another important category, helping to protect the site from cyber attacks and malware. Some examples of security plugins are Wordfence Security and Sucuri Security.

Backup plugins are essential for ensuring the security of the site's data. UpdraftPlus is a popular backup plugin that allows you to schedule automatic backups and easily restore the site in case of data loss.

Lastly, analytics plugins are useful for monitoring site performance and obtaining useful information on how to optimize it. Google Analytics is one of the most used analytics plugins, allowing you to track site traffic, conversions, and much more.

Using plugins is essential for adding functionality to the site with WordPress and improving the user experience. With a wide range of plugins available, you can customize the site according to your needs and achieve your online goals. So, do not hesitate to explore the WordPress plugin repository and take advantage of the endless possibilities offered by these tools to improve your website.

10. Search Engine Optimization (SEO)

In recent years, Search Engine Optimization (SEO) has become a fundamental element in improving the visibility and position of a website on search engines such as Google. With the advent of WordPress, one of the most widely used platforms for website creation, SEO optimization has become even more accessible and simple thanks to the use of specific plugins and various integrated features.

WordPress offers a variety of tools and plugins that allow for easy optimization of a website for search engines. Among the most popular and widely used SEO optimization plugins in WordPress are Yoast SEO, All in One SEO Pack, Rank Math, and SEOPress. These plugins offer advanced functionalities for optimizing page titles, meta descriptions, H1 tags, image optimization, and much more.

One of the first steps to optimize a WordPress website is to install and configure one of the aforementioned SEO plugins. Once the plugin is installed, you can start optimizing page meta tags, titles, descriptions, and H1 tags. These are essential elements for indicating to search engines what the content of the pages is about, and they should be carefully chosen based on the most relevant keywords for your website.

In addition to optimizing meta tags, it is important to also optimize the images on the site. WordPress allows you to add alternative text (ALT text) to images, which is crucial for indicating to search engines what the image is about. Furthermore, it is important to resize images to improve page loading time, a crucial factor for ranking on Google.

Another important aspect of SEO optimization on WordPress is the site structure. It is crucial to create a hierarchical and intuitive structure to facilitate user and search engine navigation. Using categories and tags appropriately, creating a site map, and using internal links are just some of the best practices for improving site structure and promoting better ranking on Google.

Additionally, it is important to monitor site loading speed. A fast site is essential for improving user experience and achieving better search engine rankings. WordPress offers various solutions to optimize site speed, such as image compression, reducing CSS and JavaScript files, and using caching.

Another aspect to consider for SEO optimization on WordPress is content. Quality and relevant content is essential for attracting visitors and improving Google ranking. It is important to create original, well-structured content optimized for relevant keywords in your industry. Moreover, regularly updating content and publishing new articles is advisable to keep the site fresh and interesting for users and search engines.

Finally, it is important to constantly monitor and analyze the performance of the website to evaluate the effectiveness of the SEO optimization strategies adopted. Use tools like Google Analytics and Google Search Console to track traffic, keywords, search engine positions, and other useful data to continuously improve website ranking.

Search Engine Optimization (SEO) is a continuous and fundamental process to improve the visibility and ranking of a website on Google. With WordPress and the use of specific plugins and integrated features, it is possible to easily optimize a website for search engines and improve online performance. By following best practices and constantly monitoring site performance, you can achieve excellent results and rank at the top of search results pages.

11. User and role management within WordPress

WordPress is one of the most widely used CMS (Content Management Systems) in the world for creating and managing websites. Among its many features, there is the ability to manage users and roles effectively and customarily. In this article, we will delve into how user and role management works within WordPress.

User management in WordPress allows you to create, edit, and delete user accounts that can access the site. Additionally, you can assign specific roles and permissions to them to limit or allow access to certain functionalities and resources of the site.

To access the user management section in WordPress, simply log in to the administration panel (Dashboard) and select the "Users" option from the navigation menu on the left. From here, you can view the list of all registered users and details regarding their accounts.

To add a new user, you can click on the "Add New" button and fill out the form with the required data, such as name, email address, and password. Furthermore, you can assign a specific role to the new user through the "Role" option in the creation form: administrator, editor, author, contributor, or subscriber.

Each role has predefined permissions that determine the actions a user can take within the site. For example, an administrator has full access to all functions and resources of the site, including the ability to modify WordPress settings and install plugins and themes. An editor can publish, edit, and delete articles and pages, but does not have access to the site settings.

The author role allows creating and publishing articles, but not editing those of other users. A contributor can write articles but cannot publish them, and a subscriber can only access their profile and update their information.

You can customize the permissions associated with predefined roles or create new custom roles with specific permissions through plugins like User Role Editor or Members. This way, you can precisely define the actions allowed to each type of user within the site.

User and role management in WordPress are particularly important to ensure the security and proper organization of the site. Assigning appropriate roles to users helps prevent errors and security issues, allowing everyone to carry out their activities efficiently and in compliance with the site rules.

Furthermore, user management is also useful for websites with multiple collaborators and authors, to establish who has the right to publish content and who is responsible for changes and updates. Thanks to the flexibility of WordPress, it is possible to create a user and role management system tailored to each type of website and organization.

Lastly, it is important to regularly monitor the user section to check for unauthorized or inactive accounts and to update role permissions based on the site's needs. Proper user and role management helps keep the site secure, organized, and functional for users and administrators.

User and role management in WordPress are fundamental aspects to ensure the proper functioning and security of the website. With WordPress features, you can customize user permissions and roles simply and effectively, ensuring controlled and secure access to site resources. With correct user and role organization, you can keep the website up to date, secure, and functional for all users and administrators involved.

12. Creating Custom Navigation Menus with WordPress

Creating custom navigation menus with WordPress.

To get started, log in to the control panel of your WordPress site and go to the "Appearance" section in the left menu. Here you will find the "Menu" option, which will allow you to create and customize your navigation menus.

Once in the "Menu" section, you can create a new menu by clicking the "Create a new menu" button. You can give the menu a name, such as "Main Menu" or "Footer Menu," to make it easily identifiable.

After creating the menu, you will need to add navigation items. On the left side of the page, you will see a list of all the pages on your site, the categories, and tags you have created. You can select the items you want to add to the menu and click "Add to menu."

Once all desired items have been added, you can organize and structure them as you like by simply dragging and dropping them into the desired position.

In addition to pages, categories, and tags, you can also add custom links to the navigation menu. For example, if you want to add a link to your social profile or an external page to your site, you can do so easily through the "Custom Link" option.

A very useful feature of WordPress is the ability to create multi-level navigation menus. This means you can create submenus to better organize the content of your site. To create a submenu, drag the item you want to include as a submenu under the main item and position it slightly to the right. This way, you will create a cascading structure for your navigation menu.

When you have finished creating and customizing the navigation menu, don't forget to save it by clicking the "Save menu" button in the upper right corner of the page.

Once the menu is saved, you will need to associate it with the navigation area of your site. To do this, go to the "Menu Locations" section on the main "Menu" page. Here you will see all the navigation areas available in your WordPress theme. Select the navigation area to which you want to associate the created menu and then click "Save changes."

The custom navigation menu you created will now be displayed on your WordPress site, making it easier for your visitors to navigate and improving the overall user experience.

Furthermore, you can further customize the design of the navigation menu using custom CSS or utilizing the customization options offered by your WordPress theme. For example, you can change the color, text size, link style, and much more.

Creating custom navigation menus with WordPress is a simple and effective way to organize and structure the content of your site. By following the steps described in this article, you can create intuitive and attractive navigation menus that will make the browsing experience more enjoyable for your visitors.

13. Using sidebar widgets to customize the appearance of the site with WordPress

WordPress is one of the most widely used CMS platforms in the world for creating and managing websites. Thanks to its flexibility and wide range of features offered, it is possible to customize the appearance of your site in a simple and effective way. One of the most useful tools for customizing the appearance of a WordPress site are sidebar widgets, which allow you to add dynamic and interactive elements to the sidebars of pages.

Sidebar widgets are small modules that can be inserted into the sidebars of a WordPress site to add additional functionality or customize the site's appearance. With these widgets, you can insert elements such as navigation menus, category lists, search boxes, advertising banners, social feeds, contact forms, and much more.

To use sidebar widgets on WordPress, simply access the site's administration area and go to the "Appearance" section and then "Widgets". Here you can view all available widgets and drag them into the sidebars of the chosen theme to display them on the site.
Additionally, you can customize the widgets by changing their settings and choosing where and how to display them within the site.

Sidebar widgets offer great versatility and allow you to customize the appearance of the site quickly and easily, without the need to know programming languages like HTML, CSS, or JavaScript. Furthermore, thanks to the wide range of widgets available, you can create a truly unique website that suits your needs and style.

Widgets are divided into different categories based on the functionality they offer. Among the most common and widely used widgets are:

- Navigation menu: allows you to insert a navigation menu into the sidebar of the site to facilitate navigation between pages and sections.

- Category list: displays a list of categories on the site, allowing users to filter content based on topics of interest.

- Search box: allows users to search within the site by entering a keyword in the search field.

- Social feed: displays feeds from major social networks such as Facebook, Twitter, Instagram, LinkedIn, keeping users updated on the latest news published on social media.

- Contact box: allows users to send messages directly from the site to the administrator or support team, facilitating communication between users and site managers.

- Advertising banner: allows you to insert advertising banners into the sidebar of the site to promote products, services, or events.

Additionally, there are numerous additional widgets created by independent developers and designers that can be installed and used for free or for a fee to further customize the appearance of your WordPress site. These additional widgets offer advanced functionality and attractive designs to enhance the user experience and make the site even more professional and functional.

Using sidebar widgets on WordPress is a great way to customize the appearance of your site in a simple and effective way, without the need for in-depth technical knowledge. With the wide range of widgets available and the ability to customize them according to your needs and style, you can create a unique and professional website that attracts and retains users.

14. Integration of social media on WordPress website with WordPress

Integrating social media on a WordPress website is a crucial step for any business looking to expand its online presence and interact with its audience more effectively. Social media has become an essential tool for promoting websites and engaging users through the sharing of interesting and relevant content.

WordPress, with its flexibility and user-friendly interface, offers various options to integrate social media on your website. In this article, we will explore the different ways you can do this and how to make the most of this feature to enhance user experience and increase site visibility.

One of the easiest ways to integrate social media on WordPress is by using plugins specifically designed for this purpose. There are several options available on the market that allow you to add social media sharing buttons, real-time social media feeds, and more. Some of the most popular plugins for integrating social media on WordPress include ShareThis, AddToAny, and Simple Share Buttons Adder.

To add social media sharing buttons, you can use one of these plugins and add the buttons directly to your site's pages or posts. It's important to ensure that the sharing buttons are strategically placed on the site so that users can easily share content they find interesting. Additionally, you can customize the buttons based on your site's design and user preferences, such as choosing which social networks to include and what size buttons to use.

In addition to sharing buttons, you can integrate social media feeds directly on your WordPress site. This allows users to view the latest posts from their social accounts directly on the homepage or internal pages of the site. This feature is particularly useful for promoting social profiles and encouraging users to follow the company on other platforms.

To integrate social media feeds on WordPress, you can use plugins like dedicated widgets, such as Custom Facebook Feed or Smash Balloon Social Photo Feed. These plugins allow you to customize feeds based on your site's needs, such as choosing which posts to display, what layout to use, and what filtering options to apply.

Another option to integrate social media on WordPress is to embed social network widgets directly into the site's theme. This provides more granular control over the position and design of social media feeds but requires more knowledge of WordPress code and functionality. However, this option can be advantageous for fully customizing the look and functionality of social media feeds on the site.

To embed social network widgets directly into the WordPress theme, you need to insert the appropriate code within the theme files. This may involve editing the theme's PHP files or using shortcodes to place widgets in desired locations on the site. It's important to be cautious not to compromise the design or functionality of the site during this process to avoid any display or compatibility issues.

Once social media is integrated on the WordPress site, it's important to monitor and analyze user interactions with the shared content on social networks. This can be done using tracking and analytics tools integrated into the social networks themselves or through additional plugins like Google Analytics. These tools allow you to collect data on shares, likes, and comments on social media posts to evaluate the effectiveness of your social media marketing strategy and make any necessary changes based on the results.

Integrating social media on a WordPress site is a crucial step in expanding reach and engagement with the online audience. By using dedicated plugins, real-time feeds, or embedding widgets directly into the theme, you can enhance user experience and increase site visibility on social networks. By monitoring and analyzing user interactions, you can optimize your social media marketing strategy and achieve better results in user engagement and content promotion.

15. How to Create a Funnel with WordPress

A sales funnel is a marketing process that guides potential customers through a series of steps aimed at converting them into actual customers. This process involves the use of specific content and tools to capture the visitor's attention, lead them through the funnel, and ultimately convince them to make a purchase. Creating an effective sales funnel is crucial for increasing conversions and maximizing profitability for your business.

In this article, I will explain how to create a funnel with WordPress, one of the most popular and flexible content management platforms available on the market. With the right combination of plugins and marketing strategies, you will be able to create an effective sales funnel that will increase your revenue and business success.

Step 1: Define the goals of the funnel

The first thing to do when creating a funnel with WordPress is to clearly define the goals you want to achieve. These goals may include lead generation, acquiring new customers, increasing sales, or any other specific goal for your business. Once you have a clear idea of your funnel's goals, you will be able to design a path that will lead you to successfully reach them.

Step 2: Choose the right tools and WordPress plugins

After defining your funnel's goals, it is important to choose the right tools and WordPress plugins to help you create and manage your funnel effectively. Some plugins you may consider include:

- Elementor: a powerful page builder that allows you to create custom landing pages for your funnel.

- WooCommerce: an e-commerce plugin that allows you to create an online store and manage your products and orders.

- OptinMonster: a lead generation plugin that helps you capture visitor data and convert them into qualified leads.

- Thrive Leads: another lead generation plugin that helps you create customized pop-ups and subscription forms for your funnel.

These are just a few examples of plugins you can use to create an effective funnel with WordPress. It is important to research and evaluate your specific needs to choose the right plugins that best fit your marketing strategy.

Step 3: Create an effective landing page

An effective landing page is essential for capturing visitors' attention and initiating the conversion process through the funnel. Using a page builder like Elementor, you can easily create highly customized landing pages that align with your goals and marketing strategy. Make sure your landing page is clear, professional, and attractive, and includes elements such as a catchy headline, a brief description of your product or service, a visible call-to-action, and a lead generation form.

Step 4: Create valuable content for your funnel

In addition to the landing page, it is important to create valuable content for your funnel that helps guide visitors through the conversion process. This content can include informative articles, video tutorials, webinars, podcasts, or any other type of content relevant to your target audience. Ensure your content is informative, useful, and engaging, and offers visitors solutions and answers to their specific needs and problems.

Step 5: Implement automated marketing strategies

To maximize the effectiveness of your funnel, it is important to implement automated marketing strategies that allow you to interact with visitors in a personalized and automated way. With tools like OptinMonster or Thrive Leads, you can create customized pop-ups and subscription forms that trigger based on visitor behavior, allowing you to send them special offers, promotions, and targeted messages to guide them through the sales funnel more effectively.

Step 6: Monitor and optimize your funnel

Once you have launched your funnel, it is important to closely monitor performance and results to identify any areas for improvement and optimize your funnel to maximize conversions. Using analytics tools like Google Analytics, you can monitor site traffic, conversions, traffic sources, and other key data that will help you make informed decisions and continually improve your sales funnel.

Creating a funnel with WordPress can be a complex and challenging process, but with the right strategy and tools, you will be able to create an effective funnel that will help you achieve your marketing goals and generate profits for your business. By following the steps and guidelines outlined in this article, you will be able to create a successful sales funnel that will allow you to grow and thrive in your industry.

16. WordPress Backup and Restore

Backing up and restoring a WordPress site are essential procedures to ensure the security and continuity of your website. Whether you need to migrate your site to a new server, restore a previous version of the site after making incorrect changes, or simply create a backup to avoid data loss, it is crucial to know how to properly perform a backup and restore.

The process of backing up and restoring a WordPress site can be divided into several phases, each of which requires attention and precision to avoid errors that could compromise the integrity of the site. In this detailed guide, I will show you how to perform a full backup of your WordPress site and how to effectively and safely restore the backup.

WordPress Site Backup:

1. Use a backup plugin: The first step in backing up your WordPress site is to choose a reliable backup plugin. There are many plugins available on the market, but one of the most popular and reliable ones is UpdraftPlus. To install UpdraftPlus on your site, go to "Plugins" in your WordPress admin area, click on "Add new," and search for the plugin in the search field. Once installed and activated, go to Settings -> UpdraftPlus Backup and configure the backup settings according to your preferences.

2. Perform a full backup: After setting up the backup plugin, you can initiate the first full backup of your WordPress site. Make sure to include all your site files, including the database, in the backup settings. Generally, a full backup should be done regularly to ensure that all information is securely saved.

3. Save the backup in a secure location: Once the backup is complete, it is important to save the files in a secure location, such as a remote server, a cloud storage service, or your local

computer. UpdraftPlus allows you to choose the backup storage location and set up automatic schedules for sending backups at regular intervals.

4. Verify the backup integrity: After saving the backup, it is advisable to periodically check the file integrity to ensure that there are no issues during the restore process. You can do this by opening the backup files and verifying that all information is present and correctly saved.

Restoring the WordPress Site:

1. Download the backup: Before starting the WordPress site restore, make sure you have a copy of the full backup of your site. You can download the backup from the storage location where you saved it and have it ready for the restore.

2. Disable or remove the existing site version:

Before restoring the backup, it is recommended to temporarily disable the existing site to avoid overlaps or conflicts during the restore. You can do this by disabling the cache plugin, deactivating the active theme, or putting the site in maintenance mode.

3. Use the backup plugin for restore: Once the site is disabled, you can use the backup plugin to restore the full backup of your WordPress site. Go to Settings -> UpdraftPlus Backup and select the restore option. Follow the plugin's instructions to upload the backup file and start the restore process.

4. Verify the restore: After completing the site restore, it is important to check that everything is back to normal. Check the pages, posts, images, and all site elements to ensure that there are no issues or errors during the restore.

5. Perform a security check: Finally, after completing the restore, it is advisable to

perform a security check to ensure that the site is protected from any external threats. You can install a security plugin like Wordfence to protect your site from hackers, malware, and other online attacks.

Conclusion:

Backing up and restoring a WordPress site are crucial procedures to ensure the security and continuity of your website. By following the detailed instructions in this guide and using tools like the UpdraftPlus backup plugin, you can create regular backups of your site and easily restore a previous version if needed. Always remember to save backups in secure locations and verify file integrity before performing the restore to avoid issues and data loss. With care and precision, you can ensure that your WordPress site is always protected and ready to handle any situation.

17. Optimizing website performance with WordPress

WordPress is one of the most widely used CMS platforms in the world for creating websites, thanks to its flexibility, ease of use, and wide range of available plugins and themes. However, a common issue many WordPress site owners face is slow site speed. A slow site is not only frustrating for users, but it can also harm search engine rankings and reduce conversion rates.

For this reason, optimizing website performance with WordPress is crucial to ensure an optimal user experience and improve online visibility. In this article, we will explore various techniques and strategies for optimizing WordPress site performance.

1. Hosting selection

One of the main factors influencing WordPress site performance is hosting. It is crucial to choose reliable and high-performance hosting, capable of providing fast response times and good page loading speeds. It is recommended to opt for VPS or dedicated hosting to have dedicated server resources and effectively manage site traffic and resources.

2. Image optimization

Images are often the main cause of slow websites. It is important to optimize images by uploading appropriately sized files and compressing images before publishing them on the site. There are various plugins available that allow for automatic image optimization without compromising quality, such as WP Smush or EWWW Image Optimizer.

3. Caching usage

Caching is a technique that temporarily stores website data to reduce page loading times. There are several caching plugins available for WordPress, such as WP Super Cache or W3 Total Cache, which allow for creating static page caches and improving site performance.

4. Code optimization

Clean and optimized code is essential to ensure optimal WordPress site performance. It is important to avoid excessive plugin usage, refrain from loading unnecessary scripts, and minimize external calls to the site. Tools like Query Monitor can be used to identify and optimize slow SQL queries, and WP Debug can be used to identify any code errors on the site.

5. Updating WordPress and plugins

Keeping WordPress and plugins up to date is essential to ensure site security and performance. WordPress updates often include performance improvements and bug fixes that can impact site speed. Additionally, it is important to remove unused plugins and keep only the necessary ones to avoid site overload.

6. CDN usage

A Content Delivery Network (CDN) is a useful tool for improving WordPress site performance, especially if your audience is distributed across different parts of the world. A CDN temporarily stores copies of the website on servers located in various geographic regions, reducing page loading times for users far from the main server.

7. Performance monitoring

Finally, it is important to regularly monitor WordPress site performance to identify any issues and ensure the site is functioning correctly. There are various performance monitoring tools available, such as Google PageSpeed Insights, GTmetrix, and Pingdom, which allow you to assess page loading speed, code optimization, and other key factors influencing site performance.

Optimizing website performance with WordPress is an ongoing process that requires constant attention and regular performance monitoring. By following the techniques and strategies described in this article, you can significantly improve the speed and efficiency of your WordPress site, ensuring an optimal user experience and greater online visibility.

18. Wordpress website security: protection from hacker attacks and spam

WordPress website security: protection from hacker attacks and spam

WordPress is one of the most popular CMS platforms used worldwide for creating websites. While it offers a wide range of features and ease of use, its widespread usage has made it a prime target for hackers and spammers.

Protecting a WordPress website from hacker attacks and spam is therefore a top priority for any webmaster or website owner. In this article, we will explore some of the most effective strategies and techniques to ensure the security of your WordPress website.

1. Always keep WordPress, plugins, and themes updated

One of the main entry points for hackers is vulnerabilities found in outdated versions of WordPress, plugins, and themes. Keeping all elements of your site updated is crucial to ensure its security. Make sure to regularly check for updates and install them promptly.

2. Use security plugins

There are numerous security plugins specifically designed to protect WordPress websites from hacker attacks and spam. Some of the most popular and reliable ones include Wordfence Security, Sucuri Security, and iThemes Security. These tools offer features such as site scanning, firewalls, monitoring of suspicious activities, and much more.

3. Use complex passwords

Passwords are one of the most common weak points in any security system. Make sure to use complex passwords that include uppercase and lowercase letters, numbers, and symbols. Avoid using easily guessable passwords like "123456" or "password".

4. Limit login attempts

Many hacker attacks are based on consecutive login attempts to the WordPress admin panel. To protect against these types of attacks, you can limit the number of login attempts allowed before the user's IP is blocked. If a user enters the wrong password multiple times, the system will automatically block their IP address.

5. Disable unnecessary features

WordPress offers many features and options that can be disabled if they are not strictly necessary for the site's operation. For example, you can disable user registration if you do not need it, or turn off comments on your articles if you do not want to receive spam.

6. Protect the wp-config.php file

The wp-config.php file contains the credentials for accessing your site's database and is therefore a primary target for hackers. Make sure to protect this file with appropriate web server configuration rules to prevent malicious actors from accessing your sensitive information.

7. Set directories and files properly

Ensure that you set the access permissions for directories and files of your WordPress site correctly. Directories should have permissions of 755 and files 644. Avoid granting write permissions to all users, as this could make your site vulnerable to hacker attacks.

8. Use an SSL certificate

An SSL certificate is essential to ensure that data exchanged between your site and users is encrypted and protected from malicious interceptions. Installing an SSL certificate on your WordPress site is an essential step to enhance the security and credibility of your online platform.

9. Monitor the site regularly

Lastly, it is crucial to monitor the site regularly for any suspicious activities or abnormal behaviors. Use monitoring tools provided by security plugins or external security services to keep track of the integrity of your WordPress site.

Protecting a WordPress website from hacker attacks and spam requires constant commitment and a series of preventive actions. By following the guidelines and techniques suggested in this article, you can significantly increase the security of your site and ensure optimal protection against malicious intrusion attempts.

19. Monitoring and analyzing website traffic with WordPress

Monitoring and analyzing website traffic is essential to understand how users interact with the content and to identify any issues that may compromise the user experience. With WordPress, you can use various monitoring platforms and tools to gather detailed data on site traffic and performance metrics.

One of the most popular solutions for monitoring site traffic with WordPress is Google Analytics. This tool offers a wide range of features that allow you to track user behavior, traffic sources, most visited pages, and more. To integrate Google Analytics with WordPress, simply sign up for a Google Analytics account, obtain the tracking code, and add it to the website using a dedicated plugin such as MonsterInsights or GA Google Analytics.

Once Google Analytics is properly configured

on the WordPress site, you can access the dashboard to view real-time data and analyze key metrics such as number of visits, average time spent on the site, bounce rate, and more. Additionally, you can create custom reports to monitor specific metrics or audience segments and gain more detailed insights into user behavior.

In addition to Google Analytics, there are other traffic monitoring tools that can be integrated with WordPress to obtain more detailed information on the audience and site performance. For example, platforms like SEMrush, Ahrefs, and Moz offer advanced tools for keyword analysis, competitor monitoring, and traffic quality assessment.

To gather more detailed information on user behavior and the effectiveness of marketing strategies, it is advisable to use heatmap tools such as Hotjar or Crazy Egg. These tools allow you to visually see where users click and scroll on site pages, identifying the most engaging areas and those that may require improvement.

In addition to monitoring traffic and user interaction, it is important to also keep an eye on website performance in terms of loading speed and SEO optimization. Tools like GTmetrix, Pingdom, and PageSpeed Insights provide detailed reports on site performance and suggest improvements to optimize loading speed and enhance user experience.

Finally, to monitor traffic from social media and evaluate the effectiveness of social media marketing campaigns, you can use tools like Buffer, Hootsuite, or Sprout Social. These platforms allow you to schedule and publish content on major social networks, monitor user interaction, and analyze campaign performance.

Monitoring and analyzing website traffic with WordPress is essential for optimizing user experience, improving site performance, and evaluating the effectiveness of marketing strategies. By using advanced monitoring tools and carefully analyzing the data collected, valuable insights can be obtained to optimize the site and achieve better results.

20. Creating a newsletter with WordPress

Creating a newsletter with WordPress is an effective way to connect with your audience, communicate the latest news, promote products or services, and keep your readers informed on a regular basis. With WordPress, you can leverage a range of tools and plugins that make the process of creating and managing a newsletter much simpler and more efficient.

To get started, the first thing to do is make sure you have a WordPress website already set up and running. If you don't have a website yet, you can easily create one with WordPress and choose a theme that suits your needs. Once your site is ready, you can start creating your newsletter.

The easiest way to create a newsletter with WordPress is to use a dedicated plugin. One of the most popular plugins is MailChimp, which offers a wide range of features for creating and sending newsletters. After installing and activating the plugin, you will need to create a free account on MailChimp and connect it to your WordPress site.

Once you have configured the plugin and linked your MailChimp account, you can start designing your newsletter. You can choose from a variety of pre-designed templates and customize the layout, colors, and images according to your brand. You can also add text, links, and buttons to enhance the look of your newsletter.

Once you have finished designing your newsletter, you can create a contact list within MailChimp and start collecting the email addresses of your readers. You can integrate newsletter signup forms on your WordPress site to encourage visitors to subscribe and receive your communications.

Once you have a list of subscribers, you can create and send your newsletter directly from

WordPress. MailChimp allows you to schedule the newsletter to be sent in advance, so you can schedule the delivery for a specific day and time. You can also monitor the performance of your newsletter, view open and click rates, and make any necessary changes to optimize future communications.

Additionally, you can use automation tools to create email sequences that are automatically sent to your readers based on certain triggers or actions. For example, you can send a series of welcome emails to new subscribers or send promotions or special offers based on your readers' behavior.

Creating a newsletter with WordPress is a relatively simple and cost-effective process that allows you to effectively communicate with your audience. With the help of plugins like MailChimp and other resources available on WordPress, you can create engaging and informative newsletters that help grow your business and keep your readers engaged and informed.

21. Monetizing your site with WordPress: inserting advertisements and affiliate marketing

Monetizing a website is one of the key steps to earning money through your work online. Among the various monetization methods available, two of the most common and effective tools are inserting advertisements and using affiliate marketing. In this article, we will delve into how to use WordPress to implement both of these monetization strategies on your site.

First and foremost, it is important to understand that WordPress is an extremely flexible and versatile platform that allows you to customize your site to suit your monetization needs. With a wide range of plugins and themes available, you can create a site suitable for publishing advertisements and effectively promoting affiliate products in a professional manner.

To insert advertisements on your WordPress site, you can use services from platforms like Google AdSense, Media.net, or Amazon Advertising. These platforms allow you to publish ads on your site and generate earnings based on the number of clicks or views received. Once you have created an account with one of these platforms, you can generate HTML codes to insert on your WordPress site through widgets, shortcodes, or directly within the theme code.

Another option for monetizing your site with advertisements is to make direct agreements with advertisers interested in promoting their products or services on your site. In this case, you can use plugins like Ad Inserter or Advanced Ads to manage and distribute ads effectively on your WordPress site.

As for affiliate marketing, it is a monetization strategy based on promoting third-party products through affiliate links. To use affiliate marketing on your WordPress site, you can join affiliate programs from platforms like Amazon Associates, ClickBank, ShareASale, or Commission Junction. Once you are enrolled in an affiliate program, you can obtain affiliate links to promote the products of merchants you collaborate with on your site.

To effectively manage your affiliate marketing program through WordPress, it is advisable to use plugins like ThirstyAffiliates, Pretty Links, or Amazon Affiliate for WordPress. These plugins allow you to easily manage and monitor affiliate links, as well as create "clean" affiliate links that make the promotion of affiliate products on your site more appealing and professional.

Another important aspect to consider in monetizing your site with WordPress is choosing the positions and types of advertisements to insert. It is crucial to strike a balance between displaying ads and the user experience, avoiding overloading the site with too many ads that may be intrusive to visitors. It is recommended to test different positions and ad formats to identify those that generate the highest number of clicks and earnings.

Additionally, it is important to adhere to privacy and online advertising regulations, and ensure compliance with the rules set by various advertising and affiliate marketing platforms. This includes informing site visitors about the use of cookies for personalized advertising and ensuring transparency in promoting affiliate products.

Monetizing your site with WordPress through inserting advertisements and using affiliate marketing is an effective way to earn money online. By utilizing the right strategies and tools available on the WordPress platform, you can maximize your site's earning potential and create a stable and lasting source of income.

22. Management of periodic site maintenance and security updates with WordPress

Managing the periodic maintenance of the site and security updates with WordPress is a crucial aspect to ensure the proper functioning of the site and the protection of users' sensitive data. In this article, we will delve into the importance of proper maintenance management and security updates, providing practical tips on how to perform these operations effectively.

WordPress is one of the most widely used CMS platforms in the world, used by millions of websites of all sizes and categories. Its popularity is due to its ease of use, flexibility, and wide range of plugins and themes available to customize the website. However, precisely because of its widespread use, WordPress is a target for cyber attacks that aim to exploit any security vulnerabilities to compromise the website and user data.

To protect your WordPress site from possible cyber attacks, it is essential to regularly perform site maintenance and security updates. This way, any bugs, vulnerabilities, or security holes in the core of WordPress or in the plugins and themes installed on the site can be addressed.

Periodic maintenance of a WordPress site includes a range of activities from cleaning temporary files and log files, to fixing any coding errors, to checking the integrity of the core files of WordPress and the plugins installed on the site. These activities help to keep the site efficient, fast, and secure, reducing the risks of cyber attacks and security issues.

Security updates pertain to both the WordPress core and the plugins and themes installed on the site. WordPress regularly releases new versions of the software that include security improvements and bug fixes. Similarly, plugins and themes are constantly updated by developers to enhance their functionality and security.

Regularly performing security updates is crucial to protect the WordPress site from potential cyber attacks and ensure the security of user data. However, it is important to be cautious when updating the WordPress core, plugins, and themes, as some updates may cause compatibility issues with the site's theme or other installed plugins.

To avoid these problems, it is advisable to make a full backup of the site before proceeding with security updates. This way, in case any issues arise during the updates, the site can be restored to the previous version, preventing any data loss.

Furthermore, it is important to keep an eye on the changelogs of the plugins and themes installed on the site to stay informed about the changes made in the new versions. Before updating a plugin or theme, it is recommended to read reviews from other users to check for any issues encountered after the update.

To simplify the management of maintenance and security updates with WordPress, you can use maintenance and security management plugins that automate some of the necessary operations to keep the site secure and up to date.

Among the most popular plugins for managing maintenance and security with WordPress are Wordfence Security, iThemes Security, and Sucuri Security. These plugins offer a range of useful features to protect the site from cyber attacks, monitor the integrity of files, perform regular security scans, and much more.

Additionally, there are monitoring and managed maintenance services for WordPress that handle all the necessary operations to keep the site secure and up to date, freeing the user from this task and ensuring the security and stability of the website.

Managing the periodic maintenance of the site and security updates with WordPress is crucial to protect the site from potential cyber attacks and ensure the security of user data. Regularly performing site maintenance and security updates, following best practices and using dedicated tools, is essential to keep the site efficient, fast, and secure in the long run.

23. WordPress Custom Fields

WordPress Custom Fields are a powerful tool that allows users to customize the content on their website in an advanced way. With this functionality, users can add custom fields to posts, pages, and other types of content, allowing them to input extra information and create personalized layouts and features.

WordPress Custom Fields are based on a simple key-value pair logic, where the key represents the name of the custom field and the value represents the content that you want to associate with that field. These additional fields can contain text, numbers, images, links, and other types of content, allowing users to dynamically enrich their web content in a flexible manner.

To use WordPress Custom Fields, you need to have a basic knowledge of HTML and PHP, as it often requires inserting custom code to define how and where the custom fields are displayed on the website. However, there are also plugins and visual tools that greatly simplify the process of creating and managing Custom Fields, allowing even less experienced users to fully leverage this powerful functionality.

WordPress Custom Fields can be used in multiple ways to customize and enrich the content on a website. For example, they can be used to add additional information to a post, such as the original publication date, the author's name, or the price of a product. Additionally, Custom Fields can be used to create personalized layouts, like product tabs or service listings, or to implement advanced features, such as widget customization or managing multilingual content.

Another way WordPress Custom Fields can be used is to create custom fields for custom content types. This feature allows users to define specific fields for custom content types, enabling them to create unique layouts and features for each type of content. For example, you can use Custom Fields to add custom fields to a custom content type like "Products," such as price, description, dimensions, or product images.

Furthermore, WordPress Custom Fields are extremely useful for creating multilingual websites. With plugins like WPML or Polylang, you can associate custom fields with different translations of the same content, allowing users to easily manage content in multiple languages without manually duplicating information in each language.

There are different methodologies and approaches to implement WordPress Custom Fields. One of the most common ways is to use WordPress native functions like add_post_meta(), update_post_meta(), and get_post_meta() which allow users to manage custom fields directly through PHP code. This approach is particularly useful for experienced developers who want to maximize flexibility and control over Custom Fields.

However, for less experienced users or smaller projects, dedicated plugins can be used to simplify Custom Fields management directly from the WordPress admin interface. Plugins like Advanced Custom Fields, Toolset, or Pods allow users to easily create and manage custom fields directly from the WordPress control panel without the need to write code.

Additionally, there are plugins that further extend the capabilities of WordPress Custom Fields, allowing users to create custom fields for different areas of the website, such as widgets, taxonomies, or page templates. These tools enable users to further customize their website and create unique layouts and features without the need for advanced programming knowledge.

WordPress Custom Fields are an extremely powerful and flexible tool that allows users to customize and enrich their web content in innovative and creative ways. With this functionality, you can create personalized layouts and features, manage multilingual content, and effectively and intuitively customize custom content types. With the right knowledge and tools, WordPress Custom Fields can transform an ordinary website into a unique and engaging web experience for users.

24. WordPress Comment Management

Managing comments on WordPress is a key aspect for those who run a website or blog through this platform. Comments are a way for users to interact with published content and share their opinions and feedback. However, it's important to manage them effectively to ensure that the site remains clean, safe, and respectful towards all users.

Comment management on WordPress can be done through various settings and tools available on the platform. Let's see what are the main features and tools that WordPress provides to manage comments effectively.

1. Comment settings: WordPress offers a range of settings that allow you to customize how comments are managed on the site. Among the available options, you can decide whether comments need to be approved before being published, if they should be enabled only for registered users, and if they should be displayed in chronological or reverse order. These settings can be modified in the

"Settings" > "Discussion" area of the WordPress control panel.

2. Comment moderation: WordPress allows site administrators to moderate comments in various ways. You can approve, reject, edit, or delete comments directly from the WordPress control panel. Additionally, you can set up anti-spam filters to prevent unwanted comments from being published on the site.

3. Native comment system: WordPress offers a native comment system that allows users to leave comments directly on a page or article. This system allows users to enter their name, email address, and website (optional) before submitting a comment. Site administrators can then view and manage comments directly from the WordPress control panel.

4. Comment management plugins: There are third-party plugins available that can enhance and customize comment management on WordPress. Among the most popular plugins

is Disqus, which adds advanced moderation features, comment replies, and comment voting. Other notable plugins include Akismet, which helps filter out comment spam, and CommentLuv, which rewards users who leave comments with a link to their website.

5. Comment replies: It's important to respond to user comments promptly and courteously. Users appreciate when the site owner responds to their questions or comments, and this can encourage user engagement and loyalty to the site. WordPress allows you to respond directly to comments from the control panel or from the website itself.

6. Spam management: One of the main issues related to comment management on WordPress is spam. There are numerous plugins available that can filter and block spam comments, preventing them from being published on the site. Among the most effective plugins is Akismet, which uses artificial intelligence to identify and block spam.

7. User feedback: Finally, it's important to consider user feedback to improve comment management on the site. Users can report issues or suggest improvements through comments themselves or through other contact channels. It's important to take this feedback into consideration to ensure that comment management is effective and meets the needs of users.

Managing comments on WordPress is a fundamental aspect to provide a positive experience for site users. By using WordPress's default settings, third-party plugins, and responding promptly to user comments, you can effectively and constructively manage comments. Always remember to maintain a courteous and respectful tone towards users and utilize available tools to filter and block spam.

25.WP CLI: Automating WordPress management with bash scripts

WP CLI is a command-line tool that allows WordPress developers to automate many operations for managing their website. By using bash scripts, it is possible to further extend the functionality of WP CLI and create automated procedures to simplify and speed up the maintenance work on a WordPress site.

Bash scripts are script files that contain a series of commands that can be executed by a Unix shell. When bash scripts are combined with WP CLI, powerful tools can be created to automate a wide range of tasks related to WordPress, such as creating new users, managing plugins and themes, publishing content, and much more.

There are many reasons to use bash scripts with WP CLI. One of the main benefits is the ability to save time and avoid human errors by repeating the same operations manually multiple times. With a bash script, all repetitive site management operations can be automated, saving time and effort.

Another advantage of using bash scripts with WP CLI is the flexibility and customization they offer. Bash scripts can be easily adapted to the specific needs of the website and can be modified and updated at any time to meet the site's new requirements.

Furthermore, using bash scripts with WP CLI allows for greater control over website management operations. Bash scripts offer the ability to automate complex operations and reduce the possibility of human errors, ensuring greater consistency and reliability in site maintenance operations.

To start using bash scripts with WP CLI, a basic knowledge of Unix shell and its functionalities is required. It is also advisable to have a basic knowledge of PHP and how WordPress works in order to create effective and efficient bash scripts.

There are many ways to use bash scripts with WP CLI. One of the most common ways is to create a bash script that executes a series of WP CLI commands to automate a specific site management operation.

For example, you could create a bash script that runs the following commands to update all plugins and themes on a WordPress site:

```bash
#!/bin/bash

wp plugin update --all
wp theme update --all
```

This bash script executes the `wp plugin

update --all` and `wp theme update --all` commands to update all plugins and themes on the site. This way, all plugins and themes can easily be updated with just one command.

Another example of using bash scripts with WP CLI could be creating new WordPress users. You could create a bash script that runs the following commands to create a new user with an administrator role:

```bash
#!/bin/bash

wp user create admin admin@example.com --role=administrator --user_pass=password
```

This bash script executes the `wp user create admin admin@example.com --role=administrator --user_pass=password` command to create a new WordPress user with an administrator role and the password "password". This way, new WordPress users can easily be created with specific roles and permissions.

Bash scripts with WP CLI can be used for a wide range of WordPress site management operations. Scripts can be created to perform backup operations, optimize the database, migrate the site, export and import content, and much more.

Moreover, bash scripts with WP CLI can be integrated with other tools and services to create more complex automated procedures. For example, bash scripts can be integrated with version control tools like Git to automate the site update process and the release of new features.

Using bash scripts with WP CLI is an effective way to automate WordPress site management and simplify site maintenance operations. Bash scripts offer greater flexibility, control, and customization compared to manual operations, allowing for time savings and avoiding human errors. With a basic knowledge of Unix shell and PHP, it is possible to create effective and efficient bash scripts to simplify and speed up the work of managing a WordPress site.

26. Using WordPress with Docker

WordPress is a very popular content management system (CMS) that allows you to easily create and manage a website or blog. One of the advantages of WordPress is its flexibility and the wide range of plugins and themes available that allow you to customize the site according to your needs.

Docker, on the other hand, is a containerization platform that allows you to create, deploy, and manage applications more efficiently and securely. By using Docker to run WordPress, you can isolate the development and production environment and ensure that software dependencies are managed consistently.

In this article, we will explore how to use WordPress with Docker to create a local development environment or deploy a website in production.

Prerequisites:

Before getting started, make sure you have Docker installed on your system. You can download Docker from the official website and follow the installation instructions for your operating system.

Creating a WordPress container with Docker:

The easiest way to run WordPress with Docker is to use docker-compose, a tool that allows you to define and manage multi-container services. First, create a working directory for your WordPress project and create a docker-compose.yml file inside it.

Inside the docker-compose.yml file, define the services for WordPress and the database. For example, the file could look like the following:

```
version: '3'

services:
  db:
    image: mysql:5.7
    volumes:
      - db_data:/var/lib/mysql
    restart: always
    environment:
      MYSQL_ROOT_PASSWORD: password
      MYSQL_DATABASE: wordpress
      MYSQL_USER: wordpress
      MYSQL_PASSWORD: wordpress

  wordpress:
    image: wordpress:latest
```

```
    ports:
      - "8000:80"
    volumes:
      - ./wordpress:/var/www/html
    restart: always
    environment:
      WORDPRESS_DB_HOST: db:3306
      WORDPRESS_DB_USER: wordpress
      WORDPRESS_DB_PASSWORD: wordpress
      WORDPRESS_DB_NAME: wordpress

volumes:
  db_data:
```

This docker-compose.yml file defines two services: one for the MySQL database and one for WordPress. The database service uses the official MySQL image and defines environment variables to set the root password, WordPress database, and WordPress user.

The WordPress service uses the official WordPress image and defines environment variables to connect to the MySQL database. It also maps the container's port 80 to the host system's port 8000 and mounts a volume for the WordPress directory to allow data persistence.

To start the services, run the docker-compose up command from the project directory. Docker will automatically download the necessary images and start the containers for the database and WordPress.

After starting the services, you can access the WordPress site by visiting http://localhost:8000 in the browser. Follow the instructions to complete the WordPress installation and begin customizing your site.

Customizing the WordPress container:

Once the WordPress container is up and running, you can further customize it by editing the docker-compose.yml file or using environment variables to modify the default settings.

For example, you can change the database name, MySQL user, and password by setting the environment variable values in the docker-compose.yml file:

```
services:
  db:
    environment:
      MYSQL_ROOT_PASSWORD: mypassword
      MYSQL_DATABASE: mywordpress
      MYSQL_USER: myuser
```

```
    MYSQL_PASSWORD: mypassword


  wordpress:
    environment:
      WORDPRESS_DB_USER: myuser
      WORDPRESS_DB_PASSWORD: mypassword
      WORDPRESS_DB_NAME: mywordpress
```

This way, you can customize the database settings without having to modify the image or the docker-compose.yml file.

Managing data with Docker:

By using Docker to run WordPress, you can easily manage site data using volumes. Volumes in Docker allow you to store data in a separate filesystem and ensure data persistence even if the containers are deleted or recreated.

In the docker-compose.yml file, we mounted a volume for the WordPress directory to allow data persistence for the site. Every time the WordPress container is started, the data will be stored in the volume and can be reused even if the container is deleted or recreated.

```
volumes:
  db_data:
  wordpress:
```

Additionally, you can back up site data by running the command docker-compose exec wordpress tar -czf /backup/wordpress.tar.gz /var/www/html from the project directory. This command creates a compressed backup file of the WordPress site that can be used to restore data in case of loss or corruption.

Deploying the WordPress site in production:

Once you have developed your WordPress site using Docker, you can deploy it in a production environment. There are several options for deploying the WordPress site, including using a cloud hosting service like AWS, Google Cloud, or Azure.

Before deploying the WordPress site in production, make sure you have properly configured security settings, performance, and version control of the code. You can also use tools like Docker Swarm or Kubernetes to deploy and manage containers in a cloud infrastructure.

27. The WordPress command line

WordPress is a very popular content management platform that allows users to easily create and manage websites and blogs. Although it is mainly known for its intuitive and user-friendly graphical interface, few people know that there is also a command line mode.

The command line functionality of WordPress, called WP-CLI, allows developers and administrators to perform a variety of operations without having to use the web interface. This can be useful for automating certain tasks, working more quickly on a website, or simply for those who prefer to interact with WordPress through the command line.

To start using the WordPress command line, you need to install WP-CLI on your server. It can be installed via Composer, Phar Archive, or through a package manager such as

Homebrew or apt-get, depending on the operating system in use.

Once installed, you can access all WordPress features through the command line. For example, you can create, edit, or delete posts and pages, manage users, categories, and tags, update themes and plugins, backup the database, and much more.

One of the main advantages of using the WordPress command line is the ability to automate complex or repetitive processes. For example, you can create a script that automatically updates all active plugins and themes on a website, backs up the database, and sends an email notification once the process is complete.

Furthermore, the WordPress command line allows you to work more quickly on a website, as it eliminates the need to navigate through various pages of the web interface. Just open the terminal, type the desired command, and the job is done.

Another advantage of using the WordPress command line is the ability to manage multiple websites simultaneously. With simple commands, you can perform the same operations on multiple websites without having to access each site individually.

WP-CLI also includes a series of useful commands that allow you to diagnose and resolve common issues that may occur on a WordPress site. For example, you can check the status of plugins and themes, update WordPress to the latest version, repair the database, and much more.

The WordPress command line is an extremely powerful tool that can be used to simplify and automate numerous management tasks of a WordPress site. With its wide range of commands and functionalities, it is a must-have for developers and administrators who regularly work with WordPress.

28. WordPress: self-hosted installation Vs. managed platforms

WordPress is one of the most popular CMS in the world and offers two main options for its users: self-hosted installation and the use of managed platforms. Both options have their advantages and disadvantages, and the choice between the two depends on the user's specific needs.

The self-hosted installation of WordPress offers greater control and flexibility compared to managed platforms. With this option, the user downloads the WordPress software from the official site, installs it on their own server, and manages all aspects of the platform, including customizing the design, updating plugins and themes, and managing security. This option is ideal for experienced users who want maximum control over their platform and are willing to learn how to manage all aspects of WordPress.

On the other hand, managed platforms offer a simpler solution for those who do not have the technical experience required to manage a WordPress site independently. With a managed platform, the user pays a monthly fee for a managed hosting service that takes care of all technical aspects of the site, including software updates, security, and technical support. This option is particularly suitable for those who want to focus on their site's content rather than platform maintenance.

One of the main differences between self-hosted installation and managed platforms is the level of control the user has over their platform. With self-hosted installation, the user has complete control over all aspects of the site, including WordPress files, databases, and server settings. This means the user can customize the site in any way they want, install custom plugins, and modify the source code to suit their needs.

On the other hand, with managed platforms, the user has less control over their platform, as the hosting provider takes care of most technical aspects. This can be an advantage for those who do not have technical experience or do not want to manage the site's infrastructure themselves, but it can also limit the flexibility and customization options available to the user.

Another point to consider is the site's security. With self-hosted installation, the user is responsible for the site's security and must take measures to protect it from cyber attacks and malicious code. This may require some technical knowledge and time from the user to ensure the site is always protected. On the other hand, with managed platforms, the hosting provider takes care of the site's security, ensuring it is always protected and updated with the latest security patches.

In terms of performance, there is another difference between self-hosted installation and managed platforms. With self-hosted installation, the user has complete control over server resources and can optimize the site for the best possible performance. On the other hand, with managed platforms, site performance depends on the hosting provider and shared resources with other users. This means that, in some cases, managed platforms may have lower performance compared to self-hosted installation, especially during peak traffic periods.

Finally, the costs associated with the two options must be taken into account. Self-hosted installation of WordPress requires payment for hosting and a domain, but offers greater control and flexibility compared to managed platforms. Managed platforms, on the other hand, require a monthly fee for the managed hosting service, which varies depending on the provider and features included in the package.

The choice between self-hosted installation and managed platforms depends on the user's specific needs. For those who want maximum control and flexibility over their platform, self-hosted installation is the best choice. On the other hand, for those who prefer a simpler and managed solution, managed platforms may be the ideal choice. Whatever option is chosen, it is important to carefully consider the pros and cons of both before making a decision.

Index

1. Introduction pg.4

2. Installing Wordpress on your own server pg.13

3. Initial Configuration of WordPress pg.18

4. How to use Gutenberg pg.24

5. The Media Library pg.26

6. Creating a website with Wordpress pg.29

7. Content Management: Creating Pages and Articles pg.35

8. Customizing the site appearance with themes and layouts pg.39

9. Using plugins to add functionality to the website pg.43

10. Search Engine Optimization (SEO) pg.48

11. User and role management within WordPress pg.52

12. Creating Custom Navigation Menus with WordPress pg.56

13. Using sidebar widgets to customize the appearance of the site with WordPress pg.60

14. Integration of social media on WordPress website with WordPress pg.64

15. How to Create a Funnel with WordPress pg.69

16. WordPress Backup and Restore pg.76

17. Optimizing website performance with WordPress pg.81

18. Wordpress website security: protection from hacker attacks and spam pg.86

19. Monitoring and analyzing website traffic with WordPress pg.92

20. Creating a newsletter with WordPress pg.96

21. Monetizing your site with WordPress: inserting advertisements and affiliate marketing pg.99

22. Management of periodic site maintenance and security updates with WordPress pg.103

23. WordPress Custom Fields pg.108

24. WordPress Comment Management pg.113

25. WP CLI: Automating WordPress management with bash scripts pg.117

26. Using WordPress with Docker pg.123

27. The WordPress command line pg.132

28. WordPress: self-hosted installation Vs. managed platforms pg.135

www.ingramcontent.com/pod-product-compliance
Lightning Source LLC
Chambersburg PA
CBHW071508220526
45472CB00003B/953